FLEET RIVER

PHOENIX POETS

FLEET RIVER

JAMES LONGENBACH

THE UNIVERSITY OF CHICAGO PRESS
Chicago and London

JAMES LONGENBACH is the Joseph Henry Gilmore Professor of English at the University of Rochester. He is the author of four distinguished critical studies of twentieth-century poetry, most recently *Modern Poetry after Modernism.* His first book of poems, *Threshold,* was published by the University of Chicago Press in 1998.

The University of Chicago Press, Chicago 60637
The University of Chicago Press, Ltd., London
 Published 2003
Printed in the United States of America

12 11 10 09 08 07 06 05 04 03   1 2 3 4 5

ISBN: 0-226-49269-9 (cloth)
ISBN: 0-226-49270-2 (paper)

Library of Congress Cataloging-in-Publication Data
Longenbach, James.
Fleet river / James Longenbach.
p. cm. — (Phoenix poets)
ISBN 0-226-49269-9 (alk. paper) — ISBN 0-226-49270-2 (pbk : alk. paper)
I. Title II. Series.
PS3562.O4967 F56 2003
811′. 54—dc21
2002009366

∞ The paper used in this publication meets the minimum requirements of the American National Standard for Information Sciences—Permanence of Paper for Printed Library Materials, ANSI Z39.48-1992.

for Joanna

Wonder is the first of all the passions. It has no opposite.

—DESCARTES, *The Passions of the Soul*

Contents

Acknowledgments

Grateful acknowledgment is made to the editors of publications in which versions of these poems first appeared:

Agni: "Fleet River," vol. 53, spring 2001
Boston Review: "Two Travelers"
Field: Contemporary Poetry and Poetics: "Providence," "Unspoken," no. 65, fall 2001, Oberlin College Press, Oberlin, Ohio
The Nation: "Look There"
The New Republic: "Orion"
The Paris Review: "Ascension," "Close Up," "Learning Window," "No Explanation," "Visible World" (as "The Return")
The Pedestal Magazine (www.thepedestalmagazine.com): "Overhead," "Sleepless Night"
Raritan: "Acqua Alta," "Anniversary," "Bellosguardo," "The Kearny Marshes," "The Two Together"
Salmagundi: "Ground Level," "Orphic Night"
Shenandoah: The Washington and Lee University Review: "Geese," reprinted with permission of the editor
Slate: "Photographs," "The Stranger"
The Threepenny Review: "Water Vapor"
Tikkun: "Iris"
The Yale Review: "Skin"

"Ascension" and "Visible World" also appeared in *The New American Poets*, edited by Michael Collier (Hanover, N.H.: University Press of New England, 2000).

FLEET RIVER

Visible World

Snow, rocks darker than any shadow.
We glimpsed another life
But never imagined it was ours.

Meadows made us long for the clouds.
Trails gave way to roads, roads to thoroughfares.
When we came to the river

We lay down in the weeds
As we'd been told, hungry,
But if anything the stars grew brighter

As we waited, peering
Through stalks and umbels
Across the flat ground—

Trees: mountains furred in green.
So many shades
Space seemed grafted onto time: one moment

Thick with variation and
The possibility we'd never be found.

Men toiled behind bullocks, aimless, dazed;
But when we heard them running

We buried our faces
In the mud and did not move.
Minutes, hours, they combed the field

Until one of us broke free.
They wrapped our bodies in towels,
Fed us, looked in our eyes.

Learning Window

In retrospect I'd been waiting
For years, never speaking,
Never needing to learn. I listened

To the motorbikes, fumes swirling
From the street below—so many

People, so many ways to be alive and
I'd been given one: a narrative
In which each new event subsumed

The purpose of one preceding it—no reason
Ever to look back and therefore

No impetus to look away; no need
To imagine a future because it was

Waiting, beyond my control.
So that today it seems time began
Not when you lifted me towards you

But when we met by chance
Along the Corso, your eyes a little wild,
Since after all those nights together

Circling the ramparts, pages
Turning one by one, who wouldn't

Have been puzzled by a face so lacking
In ambivalence, so unaroused
By doubt that to succumb would mean

Surrender of what over time
Allowed us to be drawn

Not only to a place where odors
Rise from streets below streets

But to each other: the capacity
To ruin what we love.

Geese

I remember the empty platform,
First geese of the year. The conductor

Waving me inside—we were moving—
And I leaned out the window as far as I could.

I remember the cold like rain on my hands
Although the sky was empty;
I couldn't have seen them

Even if they were there: geese
Collecting themselves, formations—

You were standing beneath me;
I was moving.
And when I opened my eyes

I received everything I no longer dared
To mourn the loss of: a gift
That never could be doubted since—*never, don't*

Ever look away from me—
It couldn't have been deserved.
I can't remember your face

Without remembering that moment;
First geese of the season.

Somewhere they rose together,
Shining, beautiful, and left us behind.

Sleepless Night

Walls, the willows
Higher than the house, then light—

What's holding it above me? What dream

Of sleep, what clear
Sky floated out of reach, beyond

The walls, what cry, what rustling in the leaves?

Eyes, green eyes, one night I slept
Forever: leaves
Unfurling, catkins falling

Without premonition. I felt
—There's room for one more up here—

The slender branches: clothing
On the grass and in the distance

Rubble thinning out to fields,
Little towns, the ocean rippling silently.
The moment furrowed into time

Before I entered it, dark water
Draining from the inlet, tides—

How did we survive, forever joined, forever

Apart, dawn-soaked, sidereal?

Tiny room, a tree house, wet
Leaves swirling at the screen and afterwards

A face I couldn't recognize.

Then light. The wood releasing
Light, our bodies made of light

Still bending as we sleep—
Clear sky, a brush of wings.

The light protecting us from itself.

No Explanation

To think about purpose was to indulge
In a kind of preening: so much time

Spent locked in a room not wanting
To be heard. Other people
Passed in groups of twos and threes and for once

I didn't want to get closer.
I wanted to get to where I already was

By lowering the blinds:
As if by altering the way I spoke
I could respond to what approached me

Rather than explain.
First person plural pronouns

Felt like an exaggeration of the private life.
At the same time there remained no *I*
That didn't threaten to confuse the possible

With the merely exotic.
Desk, white flowers in a vase—
I came more truly to inhabit

That apartment by leaving it behind.
And if I sacrificed the possibility of being

Understood, I didn't mind;
At night sometimes the hemlocks
Seemed as otherworldly as the stars.

I say *seemed* because I always knew
I'd exchanged one strategy
For another; it was only

Later, from a distance, that I saw
How revelation doesn't wait
For us to choose a form.

Unspoken

A market, no, a festival: carts
Of flowers. A balloon climbed slowly, tentatively,
Above 112th Street

I wish—you held out your hand—
I wish I'd never

Then flowers, children wearing masks.
Pigeons reconfiguring on the pavement, silver,
Speckled with rain, the children

Running towards us,
Abashed, as if something could happen.
Masks: hawk waiting

In the branches; the sentence
Rising until it reaches the heart—

The heart that, captured, flutters
And coos, the hand
That reaches out to hold it firm—somehow,

As if we'd been apart, we found
Each other in a crowd—*don't say it*—
And as if nothing had happened

It was still there: hovering, unsure, then taking off
Above the buildings, higher,
Beyond the cathedral.

Photographs

Two children in a snow cave laughing.

Or in leaves. The Dolomites unfolding
In the middle distance, vineyard, sheaves, and

The one—where is it?—of the missing room.
Wood bulldozed down and somewhere in the rubble

(Dark, never to be discovered) the book
We hid between the rafters and
Forgot about. For years—

Cold air blowing off the inlet, empty shells.

Men casting lines, or reeling; who could tell
From distances like these? The night

We walked almost the whole
Length of the city—blanket of smoke.

Palms above the vineyard
And a crocus sprouting inches

From the glacier and the one (who else
Would know?) of salt marsh blurred

With sky, the room behind us, unmade bed—

I threw a stone so I'd remember
What we left behind: reflections

Of a star that breaks the clouds and
Falling, meets itself—

A book of photographs where
Something lurches, then slips free.

The dead
Evaporating from the surface as we breathe.

Skin

I could have landed, coasted forever
On its untouched plains; or

Perhaps there'd been farms,
A ring of cottages.
The horses safe, corralled.

Blank surface rising
To my eyes—a wave

Now close, now far.
Old demarcations, piles of stones.
Lines signaling that once

A field was turned,
Lay fallow, fell into disuse.
Soon chestnuts filtered out the sun.

Then disappeared: a forest
Burnt to nothing and
The farms not left behind

But razed, herd roaming free,
The white grass sharp
As nails beneath their hooves

And the river rising,
Flattening out to nothing

On the soil, festered, rough—the muscle
Torn, then healing,
Then I touched the scar.

Potential Space

More than any other room the attic
Brought to mind the house where I was born:
The feeling, oddly welcome, of a space

Open to the cold outside.
A mirror stood against the flimsy
Railing at the stairs: I watched

Myself emerging from the darkness, stacks
Of boxes, broken sash cords—this

When everything beneath the floor, the chandelier
That jingled with each step, belonged
To me, owner of the world

Through which I walked.
I insulated, built
A room within that room

And every day I climbed the stairs to find it
Freshly painted, white, the carpet
Soft beneath my shoes and little doors

At the perimeter, for storage—
More than any other,
However small, however

Readily it filled the space of what might have been
More meaningful work,

I think about the room behind the walls.
Not inside, not outside,
But a space between.

Water Vapor

Whatever appeared most vagrant
Turned out in the end to be impelled

Most surely, preordained:
As if by running for water
We discovered we could breathe.

Whenever I desired unimaginable
Change, the unexpected

Moment when wind disrupts
The laurels and the most familiar
Face emerges like a stranger from the leaves,

I should have made a plan: a design
So perfectly conceived
That over time the execution

Would deport us reeling into the hands
Of someone who with good intentions

Can't fathom what we need.
But there was always air

And there was water: we spent our lives
Between them, running
Back and forth or lingering

Rarely at the moment
When one element inhabits itself

By forgetting itself completely.
Nobody chooses to be Apollo.
Water vapor, fingers sprouting leaves.

Providence

Sound of rain or smell
Of sweet bread in the street. A glance.

Graze of a sleeve—what could change us
Forever? How could we know

When every morning returns
Us to ourselves, a gift? A man

Breaks the glass, reaches
For the doorknob—night's face, forbidden,
Never meant to be seen—

And all the while we slept: raindrops

Like the seconds between
Us and what might have been

And now, as if nothing had happened, murky
Sunlight, nothing
But ourselves. Where could it be—

A night that has nothing,
Nothing to do with those we love?

Sweet bread, turn of a cheek.

Sunlight touching our faces,
Eyes, eyes opening—

Whatever robbed us while we slept
Could not be changed.

Your hair is silver again, streaked,
As when we were children.

Fleet River

House silent as the river beneath it. An anchor
—Already ancient when it was found—

Now missing. Like the river itself
Though it proved that ships once sailed farther

Even than where we live.

The white sails furled,
Unfurling; or the rows of oars, the cargo.
And the intuition of adventurers

Who—sure of nothing—
Brought it here.

Lemons, casks of resinous wine: a taste
We take for granted though at first we hated it.

Then wanted more. Then built

These streets, brick arches
Trembling beneath us,
Dark stain spreading across the wall and now

A trickle, a drop—

Some mornings by lifting a floorboard
We can see it running clear: complete

With gravel, weeds.
Fish scurrying towards the light.

The Two Together

I rarely thought about the others;
How they nestled beside us, unhurried
As persimmons dangling from the trees. Beneath us

Swollen marshes, bristling sedge.
The hammock stretched each night
To hold us so it seemed

We never grew. We touched
Our eyelids to our fingertips

To feel weeds against our thighs.
We looked to the sky
As if we'd come from nowhere

Or a house where each desire has a different room—
Each membrane matched with what would
Startle, then grow soft,
Dissolving while we slept.

We slept for years, collecting
Tastes, a tickling
From beneath our skin that could be answered only

(We imagined) by ourselves:
A dream in which existing is to want

And wanting to receive—the burden
Of not knowing the event
Beyond which nothing more will happen

Forever relieved.
We lifted ripe fruit from the grass,
Filled baskets, added rooms

And once the rafters were in place
We rarely raised our heads to look around.
But they were everywhere. I felt them

As we touched each other, running
Through the orchard after dark.

Before Time

On one or two occasions
It was different: she lingered

At the window, turned—I was
Desirable because for a moment

I was anybody. The distance
Seemed to disappear without us
Moving but more than what followed

I remember the open window.
Taxis idling by the park.
Streetlights shining

Through the hemlock and the usual sounds
Of traffic, shouts—all of it
Starkly present and at the same time

Incomplete; as if a space I'd never
Wanted had been filled

At the moment
I wanted it: branches

Swirling at the window as
Her clothing dropped
To the floor. If I have chance

To thank for this moment
I'd like to know what she deserved.

The Renaissance Frost

Silver, dusty-throated,
Soon to disappear: one lily

Weighted, drooping
Inches from another as

At night a thigh
Will graze the body sleeping next to it and

Never know; or waking, wonder
If a fire had been
Kindled, slow, one spark

—A face seen twenty years
Ago behind the apse
Of San Donato: zigzag

Where the band of terra-cotta breaks
Against the portal—dolphin,
Porphyry phoenix;

One face on the gangplank
Moving forward,
Simplified,

Asking to be seen.
Sunlight cresting the hill—

The lily upright, parched,
Accepting itself as part
Of the physical world, fuel—already

The leaves are shed, the eye

Directed to the ends
Of delicate branches.

Look There

Fields along the interstate past

Harvest, stalks, stubble—how quickly
They absorb what's left. Pumpkins

Broken in two, rain-flattened, beaten.
Seeds whose memory is roots.

And of a thousand

One—consumed, excreted—germinates.
Who knows how far from here?

A house, no lights: and look—
A scarecrow. Deer fence shadowing the road.

He knows the cries of birds
We'll never hear,
Sees ships we cannot see, the waves

Below us, crashing inaudibly.
                                        If we drive

The road continues; ground
That quickens into dormancy absorbs

Him too: a seed, a son who
Loving his body
Watched it fall away.

Orion

Stars rising like something said, something never
To be forgotten, shining forever—*look*

How still they are.

                              Blind hunter crawling
Toward sunrise, then healed.

He opened his eyes to find her waiting

—*Afraid*—and together they traveled
Lightly: requiring nothing

But a sense that the road beneath them stretched
Forever. At the edge

He entered the water, swam so far
That he became a speck: his body

Washed ashore, then raised to where we see it now—
The belt, the worn-out sword. *I'm not*

Afraid—

Except that there is nothing beneath us,
No ground without fear. The body vulnerable

—You can look at me—

The body still now, never
Changing, rising forever—*stay*—

Like something said.

Close Up

A mouth, an eye without
Connection to what entered it—
The method so successful

I might never have realized I had
A method: meticulousness

Driven by need to account for risk.
Imagine the freedom to live

Untouched by other people;
The world existing
Because at any moment

It could fall at my feet.
It was only a matter of time

Before a syntax of perspective
Reasserted itself, objects
In relation, and I understood

Why the accumulation of detail
Felt like loss. Remember

How my face looked simultaneously
Vivid and flat, the texture

Hieroglyphical—
An eyelash grown into the lid?
To know you exist

I had to imagine myself
Completely alone.

The Stranger

House quieter this morning although I know
You're here.

                    Somewhere the river: somewhere
You listening for currents

Swirling in the eel grass, taking shape: then
Footsteps, a memory—ice breaking

In shallows, rivulets, still cold. Somewhere

—When was it?—we lived above a river.
Swift, too high, so the bank looked

Dangerous, no edge or lip—I felt

A hand against my arm.
Then it slipped away: all night

The water groping and receding, sunburn, yellow wine—

Listen to the river.

                              I know it's lingering, the sound
Of a body splashing there

Alone, waiting. Who was it? Did we know?

Our eyes are cluttered, a lifetime's flotsam
Hoarded in a house we'll never leave.
                                                                        Outside

The water is frozen and the ground is hard.
Pull me down as if I were, I am

The stranger trembling in the reeds.

Overhead

Hand unclenching, fingers curling: my body
Following, the hidden entering
What held it, what it hid

And all that time
(I never looked)

Wind sifting through the attic,
Riffling pages, opening drawers—who'd known

How much I wanted to be found?
Pacing the village, hungry, cold, returning
To the only place we'd ever known: a table

Set with nothing but our hands that reached out
Gradually to touch but felt instead

A gust, a brush of wings—
Could we have known a single night
Of rapture was in fact

Our destiny, fate
Boring towards the unseen future
From the center of our lives?

We hoarded cans, pulled blankets to our chins
And waited. Woke to find the house
Blown back to sticks,

Roof splayed open to the sky
So anyone could see

I'd wished it. Anything
I hid, provisions, letters
Bound with yarn, became a lure.

Ground Level

When we lift our heads
The fragrance of the woods floats in.
And when we open our eyes—

Red berries dangling from a branch.
Smoke trails, shivers

In the grass—a chipmunk
Inching forward, then away. Once

The landscape threatened never to end.
I craved a stairway, passages

We'd know by touch: breezes
Heavy with ground-smell,
Warm, now cold, and all before us

Nothing unfamiliar—
Blanket, coals smoldering

In the grate, a thicket
Flourishing on soil we'd worked

For years, rows planted, holes
We'd plugged—but from

A different aspect: lower,
Down where anyplace we look
We also see the sky.

The Art of Craving

Because I did not want
To be heard

I made a harpsichord: glued
Horse to cheek before the wrest plank could be
Fitted and the choirs chipped;

Each plectrum
Whittled more by sound
Than sight: a music

More exacting than the years spent
Hunched above a mitered box
Of spruce and linden
Harrowing polyphony—I heard

A scurrying below the floorboards.
Mallets shifting in a drawer.
The art of craving

Tangled with the fear of being
Noticed—sounds

Too insignificant to recognize.
First subject of the F-sharp minor fugue.
First conversation, first in line. First time

I looked into an olive tree,
Scarf dangling from the branches

And I could not speak;
The instrument

Unfinished even now,
Felts unfastened to the buff stop and
The case still slender, green. I've lived

By second chances.
I have nothing
To do with harpsichords.

Acqua Alta

Air charged with sea spray, gray-green water
Welling up through drain holes
And beyond the levees

Shipwrecks, dolphins leaping
From wavetop to wavetop—exhilarating

But a waste: so much refuse unaccounted for and
(This was the annoying part) the source

Untouched—as if the mess
Were our responsibility despite
The fact that all we'd done was watch

What we were powerless to avoid.
Still, we'd enjoyed ourselves

And since it was bound to happen again
The question was not so much of cleaning up
As of learning how to take our pleasure

Somewhere else: acceptance
Of a different medium

Would allow what threatened
To dissolve the hard-won
Distance between desire and fate to be

Transformed—it didn't matter into what.
First bits of the remaining world,
A cabbage stalk, small chips

Of wood, then dolphins gamboling
Weightless through the trees.

Two Travelers

We lived to build, not to live,
And once rafters were in place we added filigree,

Reliefs: two travelers dismounting

From a single horse. The rooms
Accumulated and their edges wore away—

The lining iridescent, smooth.
We knew that *hunger is a way of persons outside windows*

The entering takes away

But we had no entrance as we had no map
For how it grew. Two travelers.

A trail widening to a road, a thoroughfare: beyond—

Tangle of seaweed, broken shells.
When we had all the room we'd ever need

We imagined a grain of sand.
Held it, rubbed until it gained

A luster: moonlight on the abraded

Cliffs behind us and the horse
Impatient as we stood aside, apart, creating

The exterior inside.

Soot Island

A village slung between two hills: the reason

For its being there long since forgotten.
Mines scraped from the earth.

Abandoned. And throughout
The forests (chestnuts

Thick again where once
The trees were cut and burnt)

Stone terraces: the tiny
Furnaces still standing in the fields—
Etruscan, Roman—I walked

Through acres of witchgrass.
Found a stone ringed once, then twice, with quartz

But nothing that had ever been
Missed: every morning

Sea grass mounding higher on the beaches,
Then swept away. Tendrils

Spouting from the gnarled
Vines, so expertly
Stunted, trained

In rows—it was never

A reason that made me happy or unhappy.
The first sip tasted of
Beryl, amethyst.

The Kearny Marshes

Here, freeway
Overhead, I furrowed, heaved
Black silt to the surface, reeds: here

The green strands of spartina.
Carp thrashing violently as if to climb on top
Of one another, here, or
Here—

I saw the bottom clearly.
Great trunks lying on their sides,
Pediments, dismantled columns

Stained by many hands.
And in the never to be repeated moment of
Light's obliquity I saw
Two figures: day

And night, one draped
In flowers, looking forward, the other
Hooded, turning away—

Who gets to change?
Who gets the life

Imagined when we're young?
I'd seen myself in heaven, peering
Over the edge of a canoe; here—

Blank surface marbleized with green: facade
Of travertine still high
Enough to shield
The noontime lull of smoke
Congealing lazily above rooftops

Like a sea, no cars,
No footsteps
In the street—ahead

Of me my older daughter having dropped
Her coat to shiver in the sun,

Her sister sleeping,
Pressed against my back.
What grows

Grows lighter, is
Distilled. I made a map

And lost it—lost
As any morning may be
Wished for, then forgotten.

Anniversary

Candlelight, a table of food. Outside

Wind brushing the palmettos.
You wandering, a child again, the one who walked

Into her future as if entering a ruin—

Columns, entablatures collapsing around you.
Then a distant hum, a roar: the Adriatic

On the other side, beyond
The drift, detritus of other lives.

Days, moonlit nights—we live our lives

Over again if we live long enough.

Rubble behind us, ocean beyond: here
The little town, brightly colored

Shacks, the bicycles, lemons ripening in the trees.

So many years ago. I'd brought
A picnic, bread and cheese: you ran

Ahead of me, I was hungry,
Experienced enough to wonder

What would happen next—

These nights, the flickering branches, even
When we walk alone, the light

—A wineglass, small
Fish breaded in their skin—

It has no opposite.

Accessible Bliss

On nights like this, dark warren
Of streets beneath me,
San Miniato luminous above, I could speak

From the center of contentment—
Neither an achievement nor
A moment of reprieve so delicate

It threatened to disappear.
The present was explicable

Because it occupied space: a circle
Rather than a line.
Or if not a circle, the point

From which it radiates: no stars
Above, no stairs beneath—
The world, no other

Way to say it, where we live.
But even as I entertained such things

I realized they weren't true;
The saying, the search

Was unavoidably temporal
And over time what gripped me
Wasn't drama but repetition: nights

Spent browsing the familiar
Lexicon, the planet
Turning imperceptibly and still

San Miniato floated weightless, sure,
No pilgrims inching forward
On hands and knees.

Orphic Night

I felt the absence of perspective—
Light shimmering above me, filtered

Through moving water; the path
Glistening, wet, grass blades
Flickering between the stones.

I felt certain of everything
Behind me: memory

Like the river's surface,
Flat, reflecting back

My face, the willows
Shifting in the breeze. I felt

Myself drawn forward,
Footsteps on marshy ground.
Clouds opening as if the sky, opaque,

Then clear, confused
What was about to happen with
A memory, the surface

Seen from underneath: dark shapes, a hull,
The moon refracted double as it rose.

Pried open, green, a pair of eyes
That watched me as I watched
Myself—it was not

Longing but the need
To look away: I turned

To you, already
Receding, restoring

The distance, and I knew
We'd be lovers forever.

Bellosguardo

To say the journey ends here

Would imply there was only
One path, almonds scattering petals

On the slopes below.
We climbed for hours but
Each glimpse of cultivated hillside was

Unfinished, incomplete.
We scanned the underbrush
For what we'd missed and sometimes

Found it, strayed—to say

The journey ends here
Would imply there was only

One person: almonds
Clinging to the branches into spring—a thousand

Narratives, some shared, some never
To be known, converging
In a landscape that by appearing

Undiscovered made the passage of time
Plausible: two children

Scampering across a backlit meadow
That we'd always known

But never seen. Pinprick
Red of the poppies growing dimmer
In the groves beneath us and above

Small traumas flickering in the twilight, needing
Never to be explained.
Scar, the hurt of belonging

Or of standing apart;

The gift of what we'd always been
Bestowed unknowingly
On someone else—how far

We traveled to exist
Together in a field; how

Selfishly I loved when we were young.
When we first touched earth

I saw tiny drifts of snow
Beside the tarmac, almond trees.

Iris

Slowly they guided us to the river.

Molehills. Ground baked hard.
A pair of crows stood motionless as stones—

Then rose, flapped lazily to the other side.

Too luscious, too slow, the river held us
Tightly. Sweat. A fever rising
Like my hands through water, large, ungainly—

How did we come here? I remember

Sun-spoked flowers, dragonflies.
A hammock dangling from the trees.
Cold water swirling from the bottom, old

But sleek, unfastening tendrils, roots,
A surface rising in the time
It takes to tell you—

Snow to river, river to mist.

They pulled themselves out first.
As if this body, mine, by falling back

Could enter what invaded it. A hole
From which I'd poke, dark messenger—

If I remembered how to speak
You'd tell me everything.

Ascension

Because there is a car there is
A field bending like arms to keep us dry.
Because there are willows

Catkins fall to cover the car, souls
Linked arm in arm along the Finchley road.

Staves and bundles, brick stacks: for all

We know, the field is long past harvest—
Pocked with footsteps, rutted
By cellar holes; as far as we see

Mountains are shadow and light.
The car rolls forward: petals

Coat the windshield and
Arms reach out to sweep them away. Once

A lamb jumped straight into the air beside the chapel.
We saw it as children, then tried to see it again.

Cottages, farms: road dividing

The field, car generating the road as it turns—
As arms beget flowers, a lake in the field

And the island floating there, serene.
Because we can't remember

What brought us here.
Because the consolation for having been

Born is being forgotten.